SPORTS THROUGHOUT HISTORY™

The History of
SOCCER

Diana Star Helmer and Thomas S. Owens

The Rosen Publishing Group's
PowerKids Press™
New York

Published in 2000 by The Rosen Publishing Group, Inc.
29 East 21st Street, New York, NY 10010

First Edition

Book Design: Michael de Guzman

Photo Credits: p. 4 © CORBIS/Bettmann; p. 7 © Kevin O. Mooney/Odyssey ; p. 8 © Art Resource; pp. 11, 19 © Popperfoto/Archive Photos; p. 12 © Michael Euler/AP Wide World; p. 13 © AP Wide World; p. 15 Agence France Presse/CORBIS-Bettmann; p. 16 UPI/CORBIS-Bettmann; p. 20 © Reuters/Sam Mircovich/Archive Photos.

Helmer, Diana Star, 1962-
    The history of soccer / by Diana Star Helmer and Thomas S. Owens.
       p.   cm.—(Sports throughout history)
    Includes index.
    Summary: Traces the sport of soccer from its reputed origin to its current level of popularity, introducing its rules, governing bodies, roles for women, and international competitions.
    ISBN 0-8239-5467-6
    1. Soccer—History—Juvenile literature. [1. Soccer—History.] I. Owens, Tom, 1960- . II. Title. III. Series: Helmer, Diana Star, 1962- Sports throughout history
GV943.25.H45 1999
796.334'09—dc21   99-17432
                                                   CIP

Manufactured in the United States of America

Contents

Heads Up!

Throughout history, people have played games in which a ball is kicked toward an **opponent's** goal. Some people think that soccer began more than a thousand years ago, when pirates attacked an English village. The villagers killed the pirates, cut off one of their heads, and kicked it around. That's the story, at least. By the year 1000, whole English villages played a soccerlike game against other villages. Teams were large, and the goals were miles apart.

◄ *Before soccer started in England, early soccerlike games were played in China and Rome around 200 B.C. This ancient Roman carving shows a soccerlike game.*

Football

In England, because soccer was played by kicking a ball with the foot, it was called football. In the 1600s, students played football against other English students. Rules were different from school to school. Some rules allowed players to kick each other. Since there was no rule to stop them, some players started grabbing the ball with their hands. Finally, in 1846, players at a school called Cambridge University met to agree on rules and write them down.

The rules that Cambridge University students wrote helped make sure that everyone would play the same way.

Name of the Game

English people traveled all over the world, taking football with them. Businessmen and sailors brought the game to Austria, Brazil, Turkey, and Russia in the 1870s and 1880s. When the English brought football to America, Americans already had a game they called football. They called the new English game association football. Later, Americans shortened the word association to assoc., and later, to soc. By 1895, Americans called the game soccer.

◄ *Although Americans changed the name of the game to soccer, people in other countries still call it football.*

The Simplest Game

To play soccer, all you need is people and a ball. Players try to put the ball into a goal without using their hands. Some people call soccer the simplest game. Anyone who has played knows that it isn't as easy as it sounds. That's why, in 1885, a group called the English Football Association decided that players should be paid. Twelve English teams joined to make soccer's first **professional league**. Today, more than 100 countries have professional soccer teams.

This professional soccer team from the United States played against teams from other countries in the 1998 soccer championship called the World Cup.

▲

The winning team gets to keep the solid gold trophy until the next World Cup, when the new winner gets to keep it.

A World of Fun

Every four years, 32 of the world's best teams **compete** for soccer's highest award, the World Cup. The **tournament** began in 1930 to allow professional teams from different countries to compete against one another. Italy and West Germany have each won three World Cups. Brazil, the first team to win three times, was given a **trophy** to keep forever. Brazil went on to win a fourth World Cup after that.

13

Winning Women

In the United States, girls used to be able to play soccer only at school and in college. In the 1920s, a women's team formed that traveled the country playing men's teams. Today, women can play professionally in a league called the "W" league. For many years, no women's world **championship** existed. Finally, the first Women's World Cup was held in China in 1991. In 1996, women's soccer became an Olympic event. The U.S. team won the first gold medal.

These women are proud to play in the Women's World Cup game. The U.S. team won the first Women's World Cup game in 1991.

Pelé

The King of Soccer

   Many people believe that the greatest soccer player of all time was a man named Pelé. Born Edson Arantes do Nascimento, Pelé helped Brazil win the 1958 World Cup when he was just 17 years old. He helped Brazil win two more times in 1962 and in 1970. In 1960, Brazil named Pelé a "national treasure." Pelé retired from Brazilian soccer and spent his last years in the sport, from 1975 to 1977, playing for the New York Cosmos.

◄ *In 21 years, Pelé played 1,324 professional games and scored 1,282 goals, including 8 goals in a single game.*

Small World

More than two million girls and boys play soccer in youth leagues in the United States. Groups like the United States Youth Soccer Association have rules and **equipment** just for kids. Youth leagues have smaller fields, balls, and goals. Games are shorter than professional games. Kids under the age of six play 32-minute games. Kids ages 6-10 play for 50 minutes. Youth team coaches try to give everyone equal playing time. Most importantly, they want everyone to have fun.

Boys and girls play together in this Los Angeles youth league.

Soccer in America

Professional soccer started in the United States in 1967. Superstar Pelé won many fans while playing in New York in the 1970s, but many fans stopped watching when Pelé stopped playing. For years, most Americans only went to soccer games if their friends or kids were in them. Then, in 1994, the World Cup tournament was held in the United States. After this, many Americans started to become interested in soccer again.

The U.S. team lost to Brazil in the 1994 World Cup, but the close score of one to zero showed that the Americans had played like champions.

The Game's Fame

In 1983, the National Soccer Hall of Fame opened its museum. Being named a "Hall of Famer" is an honor given to top soccer players from the Olympics, World Cup games, and professional leagues. The museum is in Oneonta, New York. As a fan, you can visit the Hall. As a player, you could be honored there someday.

Web Sites:

Check out this Web site on soccer:
http://www.planet-soccer.com/

Glossary

championship (CHAM-pee-un-ship) The last game of a sport's season that decides which team is the best.

compete (kum-PEET) Trying hard to win something.

equipment (uh-KWIP-mint) All the things you need to have to do an activity.

league (LEEG) A group of teams that play against each other in the same sport.

opponent (uh-POH-nint) The person or team you are playing against in a game.

professional (pruh-FEH-shuh-nul) An athlete who earns money for playing a sport.

tournament (TOOR-nuh-mint) When a large number of teams play against each other in a short amount of time.

trophy (TROH-fee) A kind of award that is often made of metal and shaped like a cup.

Index